Q-Art is run by a team of students and graduates and supported by a panel of active members from the Q-Art community. Our aim is to break down the barriers to and between various models of art education and make the workings of the contemporary art world more transparent. Our focal activity is an open crit, which we run monthly across various UK art colleges and gallery spaces for anyone to attend or present work in. We also run workshops and produce publications. Other publications by Q-Art include:

12 Gallerists: 20 Questions
– A collection of interviews with 12 London Gallerists
(Ed.1 2008) (Ed. 2 2009). (Ed. 3 2013)
ISBN: 978-0-9564355-0-7

11 Course Leaders: 20 Questions
– A collection of interviews with 11 London BA Fine Art course leaders
(Ed.1 2011). (Ed.2. 2013)
ISBN: 978-0-9564355-1-4

20 Methods: 20 Questions
– Interviews with UK art and design educators
(2013). ISBN: 978-0-9564355-3-8

This publication has been produced with support from the Higher Education Academy. With their support we also commissioned recent graduate and presenter at one of our crits, Giles Bunch, to produce an artist video on the topic of the crit. His video can be seen on our website: www.q-art.org.uk. Shorter video clips and workshops are also available on request to support teaching and learning. Interviews for this publication and supporting videos were gathered between June 2012 and June 2013.

Published in 2013 by Q-Art
www.q-art.org.uk

ISBN: 978-0-9564355-2-1

Design: Jens Dan Johansen
www.jensdanjohansen.com

Editing Assistance: Charlie Wainwright
Proof-reading: Maggie Learmonth

'Q-Art' is the trading name of Q-Art London Community Interest Company. Company No. 8587499

ART CRITS: 20 QUESTIONS

A POCKET GUIDE

CONTENTS

LIST OF CONTRIBUTORS

Alison Coward,
Founder of Bracket, A Creative Collaboration Agency

Alison James,
Associate Dean, Learning and Teaching, London College of Fashion

Alison Jones,
Lecturer in Fine Art Practice, Goldsmiths College

Alistair Payne,
Programme Leader, BA Fine Art, Glasgow School of Art

Angela Bartram,
BA Fine Art Programme Leader, University of Lincoln

Ann Hulland,
Course Director BA Fine Art, Kingston University

Arthur Watson,
Fine Art Course Director, Duncan of Jordanstone College of Art & Design

Bernadette Blair,
Emeritus Professor in Art & Design Pedagogy, Kingston University

David Moore,
Head of Sculpture, Edinburgh College of Art

Garry Barker,
BA Fine Art Course Lecturer, Leeds College of Art

Graham Crowley,
Professor of Painting, Royal College of Art 1998 – 2006

Jim Birrell,
Head of Department, Painting and Printmaking, Glasgow School of Art

Jim Hamlyn,
Subject Leader BA Photographic & Electronic Media, Gray's School of Art

Joanne Lee,
Senior Lecturer in Fine Art, Nottingham Trent University

Juan Cruz,
Director of School and Professor of Fine Art, Liverpool John Moores University

Katie Streten,
Creative Strategist, Imagination

Kelly Chorpening,
Course Leader BA Drawing, Camberwell College of Arts

Laura North,
Director, Speaking Out

Linda Lencovic,
Assistant Lecturer, University of the Arts London

Mark Dean,
Lecturer in Fine Art/ Studio Practice, Goldsmiths College

Miraj Ahmed,
Lecturer Architectural Association/ Design Fellow at Cambridge University

Nathan Chenery,
Fine Art Technical Demonstrator, York St John University

Dr Peter Day,
Course Leader BA Photography, University of Wolverhampton

Richard Bell,
BA Fine Art Programme Director, University of Leeds

Rita Keegan,
Artist

Robert Armstrong,
Head of Painting, National College of Art and Design, Dublin

Roddy Hunter,
Senior Lecturer & Head of Fine Art Programme, York St John University

Seán Cummins,
Principal Lecturer & Course Leader BA Fine Art, Nottingham Trent University

Sean Kaye,
Foundation Course Leader and Lecturer in Fine Art, Leeds College of Art

Stuart MacKenzie,
Artist/Tutor, Glasgow School of Art

NOTE: All staff were in their relative positions at the time of interview, some may have moved on since.

ACKNOWLEDGEMENTS

With thanks also to:

Abigail Jones

Allen Watson

Anne-Marie Creamer

Carolyn Bew

Christoph Raatz

David Webster

Dereck Harris

Iain Morrison

Leanne Manfredi

Linda Drew

Martin Newth

Paul Murphy

Sheila Gaffney

Stuart Bennett

Susan Orr

Video interviewees

The Q-Art team

Q-Art's current, previous and
future participants and supporters

FOREWORD

By Sarah Rowles, Director, Q-Art

The crit is a model of learning whereby artists present their work to a group in order to gain feedback on how that work is being 'read' and ways that they might develop it further. Though they might be called different names and take on different formats, crits are a part of almost every art course at further and higher level education throughout the UK.

Crits can also exist outside of the curriculum. In 2008 I set up Q-Art whilst a student and we launched a programme of open crits across London art schools. The idea was to break down the barriers between the various art colleges and provide a space where students from across colleges, courses and levels of study could meet and learn from one another. We also opened up the crits to recent graduates in order to provide them with a support network to continue developing their practice. At the same time we invited in self-trained artists, prospective students, and anyone with an interest in or curiosity for contemporary art that had not been through formal art education at further level or above. We wanted to open up the colleges and the discussions that take place in them in order to combat some of the mystery that surrounds contemporary art and its production.

Before starting Q-Art, crits were not an activity that I felt confident participating in. I faced a number of barriers getting in to art education and spent much of my time at art school feeling that I did not know enough about how to read or talk about art in comparison to my peers. It is always hard to admit when you are struggling or don't understand something, but it can seem a hundred times harder to identify the cause of this and ask for help in a discipline like art, which is all about raising questions, avoiding absolutes, and where, on the surface, everyone seems to 'get' what's going on.

Q-Art has always tried to create a space where the 'obvious' questions can be asked, believing that a full understanding of the structures we operate in can foster more equal access and help people get the most out of their art education. In June 2012 we teamed up with Commonplace[I] and Speaking

Out[II] to produce a resource that would help participants get the most out of the crit and support organisers with their facilitation of them. We received support from the Higher Education Academy to interview staff and students from art colleges around the UK on topics that include: purpose; own experiences of crits; models; barriers that people can face; and tips for over coming these barriers. The result is this pocket guide containing excerpts from interviews with the staff, and an accompanying artist video by Giles Bunch, a recent graduate and previous presenter at one of our crits. The book and the video are both organised around the aforementioned themes and we are also putting together a series of shorter video clips and workshops to further support teaching and learning.

In the first section of this pocket guide the art staff outline the purpose of the crit, when they work well, and give strong indication of why they are so pervasive. As well as supporting students to develop and learn more about themselves and their work, we find out that they are also a place to develop the skills, peer groups and habits that will support them in their later careers – in art or other arenas. In section two, 'Finding the Right Approach', we learn about the importance of tailoring the structure and format of a crit to meet the specific needs of a group, individual, or piece of work. We find out about some of the different names given to the model, discipline-specific approaches, the different places that a crit might take place, and how and why the crit format might differ across levels of study. Staff also talk about some of the variables that exist, such as group size, duration, the level of information given by the person presenting, and there is reference to the importance of time keeping.

In the third section, 'Barriers and Solutions: Motivation, Judgement and Assessment', the staff speak about the anxiety that can be caused by putting work out there for feedback from an audience. They discuss assessment, its various formats, and student perceptions of it. Then in section four, 'Barriers and Solutions: Talking about Art', the staff and industry professionals look at the many language barriers that people can face to taking part confidently in crits. These include: a lack of confidence in reading art; having English as a second language; anxieties about public speaking; dyslexia;

and dominance, silence or overuse of jargon by others in the group. They outline things that facilitators and other participants can do to support more confident and equal participation amongst all those in the group and give practical advice for reading art and speaking in public. In the final part of the pocket guide, the contributors reflect on what their own crits were like at art school, giving a fascinating insight into how things have changed.

Unlike our previous books this pocket guide is laid out thematically rather than by interview in order to provide easy navigation and comparison around recurring themes. We did however maintain our approach at the interview stage of asking 20 simple and open questions in order to gain responses that built a clear, gradual and expansive picture, first for us, and now for the reader.

Variations and approaches to the crit invent themselves all of the time. Crits also exist overseas and in other creative fields, each with their own particularities. Even where specific approaches are discussed, there is no strict formula, and as Alistair Payne of Glasgow School of Art outlines, "Each crit, as much as you want to analyse and prepare, is going to be different. It happens live". This guide therefore does not claim to provide a comprehensive or diagrammatic list of such models or formula. Instead, we hope that the examples given will prompt questions, discussion, inspiration, invention and above all confidence amongst participants and facilitators alike when approaching the crit.

I. *Commonplace* is a University of the Arts London student web platform that gives tips, advice and stories aimed at supporting new and continuing students starting at university and settling in London.

II. *Speaking Out* is an organization that helps people gain confidence in public speaking, and works with students, graduates and staff in Higher Education to embed presentation skills in the curriculum.

THE PURPOSE OF THE ART CRIT

As well as providing an opportunity for artists to gain feedback on their work and learn more about their own interests and ways of working, crits also provide all involved with an opportunity to learn from the work and perspectives of others, to develop skills in reading and talking about artwork, to think about display and what the wider context is for their work, and in many ways help people prepare for life after art school. In this chapter the staff give their views on the purpose of a crit. A few begin by defining what a crit is:

DEFINING A CRIT

- Crits are discussions around an artwork, usually produced by a student. They are an opportunity to discuss a whole range of issues, meanings, associations, references, metaphors, problems, processes and principals of fine art practice. They can range into all sorts of different areas: politics, psychology, history – you name it really! That is why they are so fascinating. But they are predominantly guided by the work that is made and brought in. *Jim Hamlyn (Gray's School of Art)*

- Work might be put up on walls, sketchbooks are usually presented, and students can request feedback on any element of the work that has been produced. *Peter Day (University of Wolverhampton)*

- Crits are the sharing of a practice and an opportunity for a practitioner to discuss their work, articulate what they have done in their work to their peers, and for those peers to then input into the further development of that work. *Bernadette Blair (Kingston University)*

- A good crit is actually a conversation. It's talking around something, through something, with something. *Miraj Ahmed (Architectural Association/ Cambridge University)*

- It's a discursive moment in a constructive forum that help students get closer to making the best art that they can make. *Ann Hulland (Kingston University)*

WHAT A CRIT IS USED FOR

GAINING CRITICAL DISTANCE ON THE WORK PRESENTED:

- The main purpose of a crit is to enable an artist to gain critical distance from their emerging work. It allows them to understand the different perspectives on their work when displayed in a particular set of the conditions. They can see how the work exists on its own terms and realise that their intention is not the thing that is primary. The artist will be able to make decisions about the work that they may have not been able to make on their own and also understand that there may be something that has happened in that process that is unexpected, that might provide a solution to a problem that they didn't know they had. *Roddy Hunter (York St John University)*

- It's so important that students get the opportunity to have their work discussed so that they get a picture of how the thing they have produced is being communicated. Students often work and work and get a very fixed idea in their heads of what they want to communicate but they lose sight of what another pair of eyes might see. *Alison Jones (Goldsmiths College)*

- Actually listening to and hearing what is said in a crit is really important. That allows them to stand back from whatever it is that they have done and equips them with the powers of critical awareness. *Stuart MacKenzie (Glasgow School of Art)*

- Crits help clarify for the student whether their work is succeeding or not – succeeding in relation to their intentions and the work's reception. This can happen in a one to one tutorial also but because the crit is more public it can introduce ideas about audience in a very practical way. *Robert Armstrong (National College of Art and Design)*

- They are a way for students to understand how others read their work and whether that matches their intentions. Often, when students first come to art school, they believe that their work is about one thing when it may turn out to be about another. They often believe that a work communicates their intention just because they had the idea. Through the crit they learn that this might not be the case and that other people may read their work very differently. *Sean Kaye (Leeds College of Art)*

- People make work in very different ways and over the three years what they make might change quite a lot. A convenor[1] is a way of testing that out and testing different strategies of making and presenting work – the two are related. So if you are showing paintings, you can show them in different ways, and that will condition the response you get. Maybe that will then condition partly how you make them. *Mark Dean (Goldsmiths College)*

1. Alternative name given to the crit on the BA Fine Art course at Goldsmiths College.

SELF-DISCOVERY:

- A good crit is about trying to find out why you do what you do. That's imperative for an artist to know. If you're going to produce a work, you have to find out where it is coming from, what your source is. *Rita Keegan (Artist)*

- Something we asked the students today was, "Are you discovering what you are interested in or what you are exploring through looking at your work?" Don't assume that you know what you are exploring from the outset and that the job of the work is to persuade everyone else of your intention. What are you learning about what you are doing? *Roddy Hunter (York St John University)*

- They support a self-realisation of intent for the student as a way to enable the progression of their work. *Angela Bartram (University of Lincoln)*

- I had a conversation with a member of staff who was running one of our workshops today. They were talking to a student who was confused and did not know what it was that they were being asked to do or what it was that they would end up with. The member of staff was explaining that actually, this is what makes the process of making art interesting, not knowing what you are going to make, inventing something not previously imagined. If you can already imagine it, maybe it does not need to be made? So I think the crit helps students to *arrive* at ideas, and to then, eventually perhaps, arrive at meaning. *Sean Kaye (Leeds College of Art)*

LEARNING FROM OTHER WAYS OF WORKING:

- Students learn from each other. The crit exposes them to very different types of work and ways of working, and new ways of thinking about how to develop ideas. *Sean Kaye (Leeds College of Art)*

- Crits can often bridge that gap between theory and practice. Say someone has a really good idea but are not sure how they are going to realize it, or say they have approached a work in one way, they may get from their peer group all of the other ways they could have approached it. Someone might say, "If I was doing that I would have done it this way". It gives them something to think about. That's not just conceptual either, it's often about ways of resolving physical problems or problems with installation i.e. "I've made this thing but I'm not really sure what I want to do with it". It can soar from the completely philosophical to the totally practical. *Arthur Watson (Duncan of Jordanstone College of Art and Design)*

LEARNING TO TALK ABOUT ART:

- Studio crits are an opportunity for students to develop skills in articulating through language, the concerns in their practice. *Richard Bell (University of Leeds)*

- The crit's main purpose is for students to become familiar with talking about their work and describing what it is that they are doing. It helps them to become fluent in understanding how to read work as well. *David Moore (Edinburgh College of Art)*

EXCHANGING KNOWLEDGE AND IDEAS:

- Crits facilitate exchange, knowledge transfer and peer learning. *Angela Bartram (University of Lincoln)*
- It's a very beneficial process for the whole group. It's also a great opportunity to pool research knowledge. Everyone in the room has got something to contribute to that big research field that develops a discourse around a students practice. *Alison Jones (Goldsmiths College)*
- There is always a sense that we are creating meaning. One of the great things about the critique is that it is a constructive and creative process and that the people engaged in it are creating something as well. It doesn't have a physical form; nonetheless it's something that involves invention, imagination and creativity. *Jim Hamlyn (Gray's School of Art)*

BUILDING A COMMUNITY:

- Sometimes the most important people students meet whilst at art school are each other. The arenas that staff construct to encourage that peer-to-peer learning and sharing of practice to take place are absolutely imperative. They are constructing a network of like-minded or non-like-minded people that will work off each other in the future once they leave art school. So the crit is really important. *Alistair Payne (Glasgow School of Art)*
- Emerging artists need to support one another. That community of peers will sustain them, particularly through those difficult first few wilderness years coming out of college. *Joanne Lee (Nottingham Trent University)*

- Crits are important because if you don't have a context for your work, if you don't have a group of peers around you, talking to you, visiting your studio, corresponding with your ideas, then your work can become utterly meaningless. It can be just floating around in a void of meaninglessness. *Alison Jones (Goldsmiths College)*

- Peer-to-peer sharing of information and support is incredibly important. An aspiration of the crit is to engender and improve that and build a community that eventually becomes self-supporting. By year three the lecturer becomes less important because the group is developing its own ideas and its own personality. *Peter Day (University of Wolverhampton)*

PREPARING FOR LIFE AFTER ART COLLEGE:

- All of that critical learning helps each artist understand their own practice and it's important that they can ask questions of their practice when they leave art school and do not have sixteen people there. So it's very much about building a professional artist with the skills to be able to go forward with their practice. *Ann Hulland (Kingston University)*

- People are not paid to talk to them about their work once they leave education, and so the critique equips them with a range of opinions and voices that they can take with them. That way they have that background experience of hearing different takes on their work and can make informed judgments post art school. *Kelly Chorpening (Camberwell College of Arts)*

- Eventually, from the experience of having all these voices in a crit, students become able to identify issues in their own work. If they identify the issue from their perspective, there is a greater chance that they are going to be able to address those issues in their own manner and develop a practice of problem solving. You then understand that as a practitioner and at mid career you'll say, "Yeah I've been through this one before, I know what happens if I take this route because I know myself, I know my creativity, I remember when I did that and now I'm going to do that". If at the end of their degree the student is still dependent on the tutor to identify the issues in their work and the remedy for it, then that's not going to be successful. The process of the crit needs to enable artists to develop confidence in their own judgement and understand the history of decision-making in their practice so that they can make those calls. *Roddy Hunter (York St John University)*

- In a discipline like sculpture you are never really working alone. You are always going to have to communicate what it is you mean to do, even when it's just talking to technicians and clients. *David Moore (Edinburgh College of Art)*

- The crit probably reflects the reality of the art world where consensus about quality of art practice is arrived at through a process involving audience, collectors, dealers, critics and so on. *Robert Armstrong (National College of Art and Design)*

- Towards the end of the course, leading up to our degree show, we formalize the crits and have students go into the exhibition space. There is an understanding that the work has to be contextualized outside of the place that it's been made in and that it has to start to enter a situation where it can be viewed as art work. As the technician it's really handy if I am there for the crit. For instance, last year the students asked if they could have a curved wall and I could say, "Well yes you can, but it has to curve this way". Having me there means that they can develop the practical and the theory stuff together. Also, as you move towards mid-career you will be talking to technicians when you are setting up exhibitions. So it's good practice to be thinking about how to talk to a technician as opposed to just a curator. *Nathan Chenery (York St John University)*

FINDING THE RIGHT APPROACH

A crit can be called different names and take on different formats. For instance, they might last 20 minutes or they might last a whole day; they can take place in a studio, an outside space or over the Internet; they can have any number of participants, be peer led or run by one or more members of staff; presenters may choose to stay silent or say something to contextualise the work; feedback might be given direct, in advance, or it may be written down or posted online; crit groups can stick together over the course of a year or more or they might interchange to include those from different disciplines, levels, or experiences.

In this chapter staff talk about some of the different models that might be used. The first section outlines how the structure of a crit might alter over a course of study to adapt to the changing needs of a group, and also looks at discipline or context specific approaches. The second section gives examples of some of the variables within these approaches, including timings and how much information a presenter gives to their audience.

DIFFERENT APPROACHES

APPROACHES BY YEAR GROUP:

Foundation level:

- At the start of the course both the projects and the crits are very short as they aim to move ideas forward quickly. They're about looking at and discussing possibilities that might be developed. In the Fine Art specialist area, the crits are composed of groups of around eight students with two members of staff for half a day. We call the first ones at this stage Ideas Forums as they can simply come with notebooks and ideas. This differentiates them from later crits where they are expected to come with works in progress – more than ideas. The work doesn't have to be finished but there has to be something that can be looked at and discussed. At this stage we also give students a document called 'An Ideas Forum and Critiques Record'.

  They get another when it comes to the final project. At the beginning of the document it explains: what crits are and what the record is for, guidelines on how to present work, how to discuss work and what may be appropriate questions to ask. For each crit they attend there are two pages. One page asks them to list the students and staff that are attending that crit and there are a series of prompts that help them to take notes on the student's work being discussed. We ask them to think about how these discussions may have a relationship to their own work, maybe in terms of artists and exhibitions that they might want to research. Then there is another section that is just about their work and the feedback that they get from other students and staff within the group. This asks them to think about: what the successful aspects of the work are; what the less successful aspects of the work are; readings of the work that may offer alternative directions, artists and source material to research; actions to take in relation to quality and refinement, quantity, planning, time management, experimentation, processes etc. So it prompts them to think about how they might record and take something away from the crit that informs how they might then proceed in the studio. *Sean Kaye (Leeds College of Art)*

BA Years 1–3: (Those interviewed in England)

- Crits differ across academic years. *Level one* need a more comfortable and 'safe' place to learn to discuss and relate to their work openly, whereas *level three* need a more strenuous and challenging experience. *Angela Bartram (University of Lincoln)*

- Crits focus on different aspects depending on where students are during the production of the work. So towards the end of the course we will focus much more on the outcome of the piece, rather than on the research or developmental side of things. *Peter Day (University of Wolverhampton)*

- It's important to define the purpose of each crit at the beginning. There is no point in having an overall idea about what the crit is about. In the first module of the first year it will be about something very different to if it's in the final part of the third year. So each crit is defined according to the need. For instance, I have just done a whole series of crits with the *first years* and they were all about potential, "What is the potential of the work?" "How far you can take it?" Then at another point, say half way through the *second year*, they might have crits that are about resolution: "What level of resolution should the work have?" "How should it engage with fixings, jointing's, fittings?" Another stage might be about presentation and other crits might be more about conceptual underpinning. The students are also asked to take notes and are given time at the end of the crit to turn them into actions, because there is no point doing the crits unless there are a series of actions afterwards. So at the core of every crit are a series of end questions: "Does this feel right to you?" "Do you feel we are talking about the right areas?" "If you went away now and carried on with these ideas would you feel happy?" We ask them to do this because in the second year we want the student to be reflecting upon the nature of their own practice. The *third year* crits are slightly different again. It is presumed by now that they're owning the work and so the onus is more on precision, how to really analyse the carrier of the information and the audience reaction to it. We ask how the work is going to be presented and what the ambition of the work is. They might have very interesting ideas occurring and we ask how far will they take them: "Does it mean that you are going to take over the whole of this or that, or build it 15 feet high?" "What is the ambition in terms of your own energy levels, in terms of how you see yourself, in terms of what it's going to be?" *Garry Barker (Leeds College of Art)*

× The *first years* begin with a kind of 'Show and Tell, where they are just trying to describe what they're doing in their work, and practise what it is like to be in a seminar situation. It's about rehearsing what they are thinking and doing and it's quite conversational and informal. Mid way through the first year there's a 'Presenting Context' session, where they present ideas and context for their practice side-by-side with their own work. The link between practice and theory is really developed here. They test a range of ideas and receive feedback from other members of their tutor group, and that one is slightly more formal. Then finally students engage in what we call a 'Show and Listen' seminar. A student presents work to a group of around twelve students and two academics for 30-45 minutes, and they don't say a thing. They participate by responding to what has been said after the event. The aim is for the rest of the group to try and interpret the work without the artist letting them know what they should think beforehand. At this stage they have hopefully begun to develop a practice and are seriously making stuff. It's then for the other people to test out the relationships between what the presenter thinks is going on in the work and what is actually in front of them. There will be people who are completely alien to the work and people who have seen the twists and turns of how it has evolved. It's important that both are involved. The people with the fresh eyes are invited to interpret the work first. *Seán Cummins and Joanne Lee (Nottingham Trent University)*

× There are three-year groups and each year group is divided into 'seminar'[2] groups of about 16 students. Each student has three or four seminars each half year and at one of those each half year they will present work. Four people present work each time and there are two members of staff present. In the *first year* it's very much about learning the language of talking about work and moving away from "I like it", "I don't like it", "I can't say anything as I'm too shy" – all quite understandable first year issues. It's about moving the group over the year to a position where they can become articulate, confident, and feel that they can comment critically on other work, ask questions, and challenge. That takes a while to learn though, to do it properly and move into a constructive space with that. In *second year* the students put up their work as if they were attempting an exhibition together and it goes public for one night. There are eight presenters in a day, two seminars a day and the twelve who are not presenting respond to the work before the presenter says anything. So they read the work, and they discuss it as if the artists were not there. That way the artist hears the immediate reactions of the group. Then the artist is invited to join in the conversation and be open to questions, feedback, and to ask things of the group. By the *third year* it becomes even more refined. The students are learning to talk with quite a lot of grounding, depth, critical awareness and contextual awareness of their practice. They are beginning to really tease out that relationship with the audience and they can set up that relationship according to whatever their practice demands. *Ann Hulland (Kingston University)*

2. Alternative name given to the crit on the BA Fine Art course at Kingston University.

- Our convenors are mixed across all three year groups. At the moment we have whole days of these, which are very intense. Eight or ten students present in a day and they each have half an hour of full attention from the rest of the group of 25-30 students and two staff. In the past there were twice as many students. There are a group of three tutor groups, three staff and they all rotate so that one week a section from one of the tutor groups will present and the next week another will. They get a chance to see each other's work and they stay together as a group. We hope that the questions, themes and topics that come up will be connected over the weeks so that the same group will be talking and developing ideas together. *Alison Jones and Mark Dean (Goldsmiths College)*

BA Years 1–4 (Those interviewed in Ireland):

- There are different types of crits at different stages of the student experience. Currently year one is handled by a dedicated first year staff and students arrive to us in the painting department in year 2. *Year 2* crits occur regularly, every three to five weeks, at the end of projects. Students will speak about the work they have created during the project to the assembled group of about 25 and one or two tutors. The main purpose of these crits is to introduce students to the idea of speaking publicly about their work. Students are encouraged to comment on each other's work in a supportive atmosphere. At this stage some students are shy and the staff will endeavour to draw them out so that they gain in confidence and will be more comfortable with the process in future years. The idea of peer learning is present from an early stage and the students' comments are as crucial or maybe more crucial to the process than the 'pearls of wisdom' offered by the tutors. *Year 3* crits are often with smaller groups of six or seven students and a tutor. They are more focused and look at the work in more depth and with more criticality.

The student voice here is still very important. In *Year 4* three students each week make individual presentations to the entire group of 25 students and two staff members. These crits focus on the work being pursued by the students, subject area, intentionality, and awareness of approaches to similar subject matter employed by other artists. Questions of 'influence' arise but efforts are made to minimize superficial stylistic comparisons in favour of essential driving imperatives and appropriateness of material form to content. *Robert Armstrong (National College of Art and Design)*

BA Years 1–4 (Those interviewed in Scotland):

- In the early years crits will involve a big group speaking for a short time. They move around the studios so that it's never focusing on one person for too long. Now, in my fourth year tutorial group, I have eleven students that I split into two groups and that crit session with five students may go on for three hours. We do that a couple of times a semester. It goes on for that length of time because that's how long they want to speak about work for. I don't set a time but I do allow for plenty of it because if it's a good discussion the last thing I want to do is to cut it short. *Arthur Watson (Duncan of Jordanstone College of Art and Design)*

- Usually crits are done in manageable groups of about 20 students. First years have specific project briefs and our first question might be, "Would anyone like to open up by saying how you found the project and what your experience has been?" We wouldn't pick people out, as somebody is usually quite happy to volunteer. If not, the staff might prompt a little bit by asking something like, "Do you think that going out into the city has been valuable, what have you learned from that?" Normally, a response to that triggers a discussion and that's always best rather than it being too diagrammatic. The students would also be going to the library and developing research around the approach to handling that project and so it's quite conceivable that the discussion would be around the materials or the kind of things that they used for their work. Then there would be some kind of conclusion towards the end of the crit, like, "What is it that you think that you have learned from this experience that you can use in terms of what the next project brief might be?" There is more staff support in the early stages of the course and as you move through you get to a point in the third and fourth year where students can lead crits as they gain in confidence. *Stuart MacKenzie and Jim Birrell (Glasgow School of Art)*

× We do different crits from first to final year, which change emphasis year on year. In the *first year* students do short projects. We know that they are not used to speaking and that they have not really had enough time to complete work, so we start off by getting them to talk about what they did not have time to finish. We ask what they might want to do so that they are projecting further ahead than the object in front of them. This means that they don't feel a pressure to succeed, as we're only talking about the works potential. It also means that we can start to introduce the language of form and introduce larger concepts to do with contemporary art as we talk about where this might be or what it might look like in a different situation.

In the *second year* we have five-week projects and we do crits early in the fourth week where we discuss what they might do to finish. The student will introduce the work and tell the story of how they came to where they are, without any onus on them to overload it with concept or anything. Again we talk about where the work could go. It's another scenario where they are not getting something wrong as we're only talking about what something *could* be. It's not a case of saying, "You could have done this". It's, "Did you think about doing this? Because now you can do it." And so they take it forward.

In the *third year* we do outside projects and they work collaboratively. They team up and they build on the dialogue they have had with each other over the first and second year. They know each other's work quite well, what each other is capable of, and so they discuss that in groups. They discuss what their capabilities are and decide what its possible for them to do together. Then they choose a location, respond to that location, create a poster, and invite everyone along to an event. The students who are going to be doing it next go and they pay attention and take notes on what these students have done in this event or performance. This happens on a Thursday afternoon, we meet up again on the Friday, and those students that have been observing the crit feedback to the students that have just done it. Then because they are going to go next week, they present their ideas for that to the group that have just been who can then say to them, "Right, well you pointed out to us that everyone got bored waiting around, and you're about to set up and do the same thing. You should think about that." So it's like a relay where they are passing on the baton. They have got a role in observing the event, feeding forward or feeding back.

Then there's our *final-year* crits. In these, three students set up work and I will come in and speak to them for half an hour about the work and say what my first reactions are to it. I will not have seen the work before at all. Those three students then go away and the three final year students that are going to be presenting next week, come in to look at the work with three third year students from the year below. So we get a crossover from the year below and the final year. I then go around with them for an hour and try to read and figure out what's going on. They have to come up with three things that they think are working that are positive, and three things that they feel ought to be addressed. Then the three students come back in and we ask them not to say anything during what's been said and at the end to respond or not. They may just say, "Thank you very much, I'll take that away and think about it". Or they might give an answer to a question that came up. A large part of that crit it about reading work and developing the language skills to talk about work that's not their own. Often if you're just talking about your own work, you tend to be quite defensive and so you don't always listen to what's being said. However, they actually learn a lot from discussing other student's work because it's very much externalized, it's very out there, and they get the opportunity to be much more frank about it when the students are not there. *David Moore (Edinburgh College of Art)*

DISCIPLINE-SPECIFIC APPROACHES:

- A former Director of NCAD [National College of Art and Design, Dublin], himself a painter but also a 'performer', often became exasperated with staff who 'just didn't get it' in relation to painting. I know this feeling very well! But the thing is that painters can be very enthusiastic about other forms of practice, and sometimes it does not flow the other way. I think things have moved way beyond conceptual one-up-man-ship in this area and that a dis-inclination to engage with painting practices is just lazy. A difficulty arises on the subject of materiality of painting practice. Painters often do think through the material, or accept the medium as a given, while others are more concerned with the content irrespective of medium. This places an onus on painters to articulate their practice in the wider field and this is a good thing. *Robert Armstrong (National College of Art and Design)*

- I think sculpture students are always more vociferous in crits than other areas because we always talk about how to do something. Even if you want to move something you have to ask somebody to help you, so there is dialogue right from the start. When I started doing crits, they were not widespread through the college, but the two areas which became the most comfortable with that way of discussing work were sculpture and architecture students. I think that's because they have to do presentations and talk to clients to show them what they are trying to achieve. *David Moore (Edinburgh College of Art)*

- I do enjoy doing crits across disciplines but at the same time, you cannot quite get the understanding and depth. In sculpture we are very much interested in the work's presence, its effect on the audience, the role of the audience and how you engage with it. A painter might take a 3D object and use it as a vehicle to create a composition, which is very much about painterly concerns. We might be thinking about why they have used that particular object and how something sits in space. It's really important that once you have learned to talk about your own discipline, that's transferable, and that you can share the concerns that you have, as well as learning more about how others see the world. *David Moore (Edinburgh College of Art)*

CONTEXT-SPECIFIC APPROACHES:

- Each person's work demands a different type of attention. A student recently invited everyone back to her kitchen in Deptford. Everyone piled into a domestic space and she played a guitar at the table. *Alison Jones (Goldsmiths College)*

- Sculpture and Environmental Art do a lot of crits in Glasgow city centre. They might go and do an interactive installation collaboratively as a group, discuss it, and then ask the public in to discuss it with them. So they open out that critique to the public, to other people in the city. *Alistair Payne (Glasgow School of Art)*

- People respond to the specific context and make presentations that are cognisant of the social situation that they are in. One of the conditioning factors of the crit is that people turn up and have a time slot. There was one student who waited outside for about half the period and then came in. The discussion was then around their absence. *Mark Dean (Goldsmiths College)*

- There can be issues around how durational or sight-specific work is shown. We do 'Show and Listens' in seminar spaces and some show documentation of work intended for outside contexts. But there are questions about the effectiveness of that as some students are quite alert to *who* the thing they are making is for. *Joanne Lee (Nottingham Trent University)*

- A problem with crits can be that if your work isn't gallery-based you have to show documentation and it can be very difficult to avoid the discussion becoming about the presentation strategy you deployed within the space you're showing it in. So something we do is make direct use of the building and get students to make, install and then crit a work all in the space of a day. Myself, another member of staff, and a technician run these. We meet in the morning with six or seven students and we have half an hour to discuss what they're going to do. We suggest some things and then we go off for fifteen minutes, come back, ask what people need, assign spaces and just start working with them very practically. We might say, "go and get some projectors" and really kind of chivvy them to do something. If you deploy people around the building it does lead people to go "oh well there's a screen there, I'm just going to use that". People realise that they can create some kind of work in an hour and a half. They install it up until 1.30pm and then rest of the year come in and one by one we discuss the work people have done. The work hasn't always been great but it has been successful and I think the students have found it very useful. It's about not over thinking stuff. It's about talking. We can say, "Do you know how video's shown, about staging, projections and how you could scale that up?" It doesn't look like much but when in a morning you think of something, edit it, play with the scale, it's an awful lot of learning that happens in a short period of time. *Juan Cruz (Liverpool John Moores University)*

VARIABLES OF THE CRIT

Within any model or approach to running the crit there are also many variables. The staff discuss the impact of time keeping as well as how much information a presenter chooses to give to the group:

TIME KEEPING:

- One of the problems we sometimes have when there is a long schedule of presentations, is that for the first few you have a room full of people and but that dwindles until at the end you just have the last willing committed students that bother. *Alison James (London College of Fashion)*

- You have to give enough time to each individual so that they don't feel that their work is being discussed on a superficial level. Nevertheless, as the crits go on the students will get tired and attention spans get shorter. That's something that we need to build back up through seminars and make sure that what's said is significant, not rambling. It's not helped by the fact that students are spending more time on screens, in a virtual environment, and less time developing interactive social skills. *Ann Hulland (Kingston University)*

- There are practical things like the running order. People are showing very different work and have very different needs. It might be that someone needs to go after a break because they have to set up a load of props or they are going to go off-site. There is also a nominated timekeeper and someone with a key to set up before. *Mark Dean (Goldsmiths College)*

- The person being critted has got a time limit to present and we are quite clear about that because if each crit has 20 minutes, and they spend 15 minutes actually presenting what they have got, they only have 5 minutes for feedback. So we try to be very clear about timing, and at 20 minutes the crit stops. *Garry Barker (Leeds College of Art)*

'SILENT' CRITS:

- We don't allow the student who has made the work being discussed to speak about their work initially. Instead we ask the other students and staff in the group to discuss the work. We find that when we allow students to talk about their own work, they say "I did this, and this means this, and I did that for this reason", and the other students say "Oh yeah, I can see that now". They stop reading the work and just listen to the description of the student's intentions and try to read those intentions into the work. *Sean Kaye (Leeds College of Art)*

- We have conversations at the start of each year about whether we should do silent convenors where students don't talk about the work they are showing, or whether we should insist that they do a short presentation on the ideas that inform the work before they open it up for general discussion. I'm quite flexible about that. Some people are very committed to either of those things, but I'm flexible. I just think that art develops and that it has its different needs at different stages. I think sometimes a silent convenor is absolutely appropriate, whereas at other times students should actually say something very pointed about what they're doing. *Alison Jones (Goldsmiths College)*

BARRIERS AND SOLUTIONS: MOTIVATION, JUDGEMENT AND ASSESSMENT

There are a number of things that can prevent people from taking part confidently in crits or getting the most out of them. This chapter looks at the anxiety that comes about as a direct result of putting work out there for group feedback. Where this exists around peer review, the staff talk about the importance of facilitating a safe yet also constructive environment. Where this exists around assessment, staff look at the various models of assessment they use, both formal and informal, discuss the ways in which student perceptions of assessment are influenced, and suggest ways to help combat some of the anxiety that surrounds it.

KNOWING WHAT TO EXPECT

Being unsure of what the purpose of any given crit is can cause anxiety. Here the staff talk about ways that they support understanding and ownership of crits amongst participants:

- Students can really struggle with not being sure what the point of the crit is or what they are supposed to do or say. Is what they are going to say stupid sounding? Are they going to make an idiot of themselves? Is their work bad? A bit of structure can help people understand what the boundaries are that they are working within, and can help ease anxiety. To do this I like to give students the opportunity to come up with ground rules as a class. Some common ones are 'be polite' or 'be considerate' but I have also had students say that they want to see how their piece is viewed from the outside and so wanted a rule for their crit that the artist couldn't talk about the work and would just have to just listen to what is being said. This helps to give students more control, take ownership of their learning and allows them to figure out how they can use the crit as a useful learning tool. It also gives them the experience of how to set up and run crits for themselves – a vital skill for maintaining artistic practice after education. *Linda Lencovic (University of the Arts London)*

- I spend time explaining the process of the crit beforehand to give students a sense of expectations. I say, "Well it's your project and you are in control of it. What you are really doing now is using the group as a focus group, as a way of testing out ideas, of what it is that you are doing". *Peter Day (University of Wolverhampton)*

- We have a module in the first year where we prepare for the first crit. Over three sessions we look at the history of the crit and the history of academies and art schools. We ask what these are for, where they have come from, why we do these things, and what their idea of being at art school is about. We also get them to do exercises. For example, the first year students will do some crits that are not with their own work. We combine them with artist research tasks. Someone will decide to be Yves Klein, someone will be Tracey Emin, and we'll have a crit with these eminent artists. They work from their knowledge of what they found out about these artists and imagine their intention etc. Sometimes we recommend that they use the work of an artist they don't like. It can often be the case that by researching and representing their work in a crit, they gain an appreciation of them. I am also keen to prepare students for crits through tutorials. I get them to think quite strategically about how they are going to use the crit and about how many crits there may be in the course of preparing work, in today's case, for a degree show exhibition. *Roddy Hunter (York St John University)*

- We agree with the student audience and the individual being critted what the importance of that particular crit is. There is no point in the group saying to the student, "You've not got enough ideas" if actually what they need to do is think about the work's finish. And so the person being critted should say at the start, "The side of the work I would like us to focus on is this". If a student sits in front of a whole group of people and at the end of it they say, "Well that wasn't really what I'm worried about", then it's a bit of a useless crit. So the general aim of the crit is for the student to come to a deeper understanding of their work, but it has to be very purposeful. *Garry Barker (Leeds College of Art)*

- It's important to explain to people why a crit is happening. Never have the situation where you have the wrong type of unknown in a crit situation where one student has learnt and another has been left confused by it. *Stuart MacKenzie (Glasgow School of Art)*

- We try to be clear to the students about what we are expecting and their recurrent participation in these seminars throughout the course allows them to become more confident. *Seán Cummins (Nottingham Trent University)*

- Students often feel that they don't really understand what is expected of them. They try to guess what we are all about: What do you *really* mean? What is this *really* about? Why can't you be more direct? But it's not quite as simple as that. It's not that we don't know, but it's not about coming up with answers, it's about them identifying and clarifying questions. You can't just tell someone "Ok, the questions you should be thinking about are these and these are the answers, do that and you will pass". That's not what the subject is about. I think that people that teach art are also defending a space where it's ok not to know, for students not to know. This means that we can all join in this place of asking questions productively, which I think is what art is about. It's very common that we would get students one way or another saying "I really don't understand whets going on, I feel a bit lost". We have to pastorally support them through that. They might look to the staff as experts, and on some level I suppose we are, but fundamentally what we are expert at is having already been through or lived within this situation of not quite knowing. So we are trying to help them learn how to do that for themselves. And unfortunately you can't just write it on a piece of paper and give it to them. That would diminish the level of the whole thing. *Mark Dean (Goldsmiths College)*

PUTTING YOURSELF OUT THERE

The anxiety conjured as a result of putting yourself and your work in front of an audience – and ways that staff can facilitate a constructive and supportive environment:

- The crit environment seems to heighten this notion of being exposed especially as within art and design there is a lot of personalized work that comes from you or is about you. It's almost the equivalent of a psychiatrist's couch. You are opening yourself up to an audience of people that you have got all sorts of relationships with. They are not just fellow students, they could be friends, partners, people you don't get on with, people you do get on with, people you respect, people you don't respect. It's a very loaded drama, psychodrama almost! For some students, if someone is very critical about their work it can feel like someone has been very critical about them – the distance between the student and their work disappears. *Peter Day (University of Wolverhampton)*

- In terms of student care, it's important that the personal tutor is there. Sometimes people make work out of quite personal trauma and it's important that there is someone there that understands the background of that. *Seán Cummins (Nottingham Trent University)*

- You are trying to construct a supportive learning environment for the student. It's really important for the staff member who is present to be aware of the dynamic and how that dynamic is shifting. As positive as I see the whole notion of crits and critical debate, it can go dramatically wrong very quickly. The facilitation is not so much about asking questions continuously, it's watching what is happening, being in control of that environment, and allowing the students to enjoy and get the most out of it. *Alistair Payne (Glasgow School of Art)*

- The same question could be asked in two different ways in terms of how it's delivered. One could create a situation where somebody becomes defensive in some way and that should not happen. It should be done with more of a sense to enquire and allow curiosity in terms of response. *Stuart MacKenzie (Glasgow School of Art)*

- One of the tips I give to people is try not to be too defensive. Sometimes I see people defending themselves and they get through the half hour and heave a huge sigh of relief at the end of it. They go and sit back down in the crowd, the next person comes up, and five minutes after they had finished you could see their sort of "Ha, I got through that". But it's like deflation, it's almost like you can read their mind and that they are sitting there thinking, "Oh dear, I did not really need to do that, what I defended myself from was the opportunity of really opening up my work. And now I wish I had done it differently". *Mark Dean (Goldsmiths College)*

- Students invest an enormous amount in their work and I think in education generally there is a lot invested. People hope to, and often do, have their lives changed by education. And I think we have to tread extremely carefully when we are critical because so much is invested. There are a number of times where I have seen members of staff be particularly tactless in critiques. There was a time when in a crit I thought I was being tactful-ish, frank-ish, but I spoke to the student afterwards and they said they didn't mind what I'd said although they would have preferred if I'd done it in private. That was a real lesson for me. *Jim Hamlyn (Gray's School of Art)*

- The very first crit is led by staff with the idea being that they model the sort of questions students might ask. We also introduce ethics. It's not about you being critical of someone's work or saying, "well that doesn't work does it?" It's actually about building up the potential of that person to succeed. So the very first crits are done as a model and we ask the students to take over from that model so that they use similar behavioural patterns. *Garry Barker (Leeds College of Art)*

- We talk to them initially about why we do crits, what they are, and that they are critical but in a supportive, positive way. We tell them that it's not a forum to attack someone, nor is it a forum to pat everyone on the head and say, "that's really good". We talk about the appropriate behaviour we expect within the crit. *Sean Kaye (Leeds College of Art)*

- If a crit veers towards a cosy consensus, it is probably not much good. Students are usually generous when asked to comment on each other's work, but to move beyond someone saying something is 'nice' requires the facilitator to direct the discussion towards wider contexts and greater ambitions for individual works. I think that the facilitator should be alert to moments when the discussion is leading to interesting revelations or insights and should try to direct the crit accordingly. *Robert Armstrong (National College of Art and Design)*

- As a way of generating argument and stopping crits being too polite and friendly, a colleague of mine had the idea to introduce a devil's advocate card where you hand it to someone and they create the argument against something. You can also do the opposite to ensure that somebody is recognising the positive, because often in a critique we tend to focus on all of the things that are wrong or could be done differently, at the cost of not pointing out what is good, what is working. *Kelly Chorpening (Camberwell College of Arts)*

- You can use a 'criticism sandwich' where you give some positive feedback, then some constructive or negative feedback, and then something positive again. *Laura North (Speaking Out)*

- The more you get to know a group of students, the more comfortable it can be. But there can be a tendency towards what is called "group think", where groups reinforce their own judgements and assumptions. It's quite good in establishing relationships and a sense of a team but one has to watch that comfortableness because it's often quite unhealthy and could be a sign that you're not challenging yourselves as much as you could. I play devil's advocate and ask a series of provocative questions about work to stir things up a bit. Some of the groups that are the most productive are the ones where there is a dissenter or diversity of opinions and backgrounds. *Jim Hamlyn (Gray's School of Art)*

- It's a subject where you have to deal with doubt positively. There will never *not* be doubt as it's inherent in the subject and if you could eliminate doubt we would not be doing it. I think it's very important to talk about it and make students aware that everyone feels it and that the people teaching them have the same fears of putting work into an exhibition as they do: will it be understood, will people like it, is it relevant? The same fears are there no matter what stage you are at in the creative process. It's just that the younger you are in the process, the more overwhelmed you are with it. Teaching structures have to acknowledge doubt but not eliminate it, and not pump it up by making the crits horrible encounters. Anxieties are inevitable, maybe even valuable, because if students can formulate them in their discussions they gain more control of them. Often anxiety means that you actually care. *Ann Hulland (Kingston University)*

- We have second and third year mentors now to mentor any students in the first year that feel unsure or want some advice. They are a fantastically supportive group. They have been looking at their own experience of convenors and tutorials and have been running these sessions that have hilarious posters. They had one for convenors that had this very funny picture of someone in agony saying 'Convenor agony? Come to the meeting'. So there is a lot of student support going on which is really great. *Alison Jones (Goldsmiths College)*

- A lot of the barriers revolve around people's sense of inferiority, where they feel as though they are in a situation where other people are superior in some way, or have superior access, knowledge, understanding or articulacy. Sometimes there is not a lot you can do to overcome these things other than to have an awareness that they exist and an awareness that people actually rise to challenges and often do. It's about keeping the challenge at the pitch where it does not overwhelm them. *Jim Hamlyn (Gray's School of Art)*

- We learn best when we are challenged almost to the point of being overcome by the difficulties. When we are bored we have more skills than we need for the task at hand. When we are overwhelmed, at the point of anxiety, we don't have enough skills to be able to do the task optimally. The ideal – what's called a 'flow state' – is where we have enough skill and we are immersed in what we are doing. It's important for learning to be difficult, yet there is more and more emphasis on making things easy for people and reducing the difficulty. Reducing anxiety as much as possible is important, but it should nonetheless be there. I don't mean that from a sadistic point of view but because it's been proven, over and over, that we learn most when pushed to our limits. I've experienced it too. At the moment I'm installing a woodburning stove at home, partly because I've done a lot of DIY in the past, and partly because we can't really afford to do it any other way. And so we are just going through each stage just looking at what we've got to do, and saying, "can we do this?" But then once you're chipping a bit of concrete away you realize that you can, and then that you can also do the next thing and the next. So yeah, I'm probably good at installing wood stoves now! But at the beginning I was petrified by the idea. It's really gratifying as well when you do it. Difficulties and challenges are vital. *Jim Hamlyn (Gray's School of Art)*

DEVELOPING INDEPENDENCE

Using the crit as a model to foster independent learning away from dependency on a tutor or motivation by grades/rewards:

- There are two types of motivation: intrinsic – where you decide to do something for its own sake, and extrinsic – where you do something through expectation of a reward of some kind. The reward might be marks. Studies have looked at this and it is a little contested but they indicate that the more you encourage extrinsic motivation, the more you reduce all of the things that we most value within art education, especially that desire to make art for its own sake. So the less emphasis that we place on marks and grades the better. To a large degree, most courses do tend to have few instances where they dish out marks, usually the end of a term or year. The rest of the time the focus tends to be on feedback. It's pretty detrimental to give people the mark and the feedback because students tend to focus on the mark. I did a little experiment once. We have assessment sheets here that have a mark on the front and feedback on the back. When I gave them out I handed them all of their sheets upside down so that they got feedback first. All but one of them turned it over and looked at their mark before reading the feedback. *Jim Hamlyn (Gray's School of Art)*

- If a student is feeling pressured into making work, that's not right. If they are trying to answer what they think the educational outcomes of the module are, that can be a great mistake because the reality is that you get higher marks if you completely own what you are doing. We are trying to break through all of that to get to a point of self-awareness and knowing. *Garry Barker (Leeds College of Art)*

- The crit is doing something discursive, you are having this very aspirational conversation and the group go off into all sorts of different directions, and yet a lot of our students are asking how it improves their grade or what they need to do to get a first. Many are coming from curriculums at other levels where there are quite clearly defined stepping-stones to grades and achievement, whereas within a crit you won't mention grades. I think it's incredibly important that students realise the importance and significance of feedback in the crits and how they are different to what they are in college or school. There is an expectation that the student becomes independent within the process. And I suppose the question is how that's managed. How do you move from someone who may be dependent on a single teacher that guides, takes you through, offers advice, sets tasks and is there every session, to an independent learner in a university and then career environment? *Peter Day (University of Wolverhampton)*

- The really serious issue is the idea of approval and disapproval. When meeting somebody for a tutorial, who you may never meet again, they maybe very nervous. It's vitally important that if a tutor is going to have a conversation with somebody about their work, their value systems and a sense of their self-worth, then they do not go in there lightly! Nor should a tutor expect control. When I do a crit or a tutorial for the first time, I reassure the student that I'm not going to approve or disapprove of their work. That does not mean to say that the conversation is going to be without value. Sometimes a tutor will tell a student whether they "like" their work or not, even if they do so in a sophisticated or coded way. I attempt to take that out of the equation. We have got to get away from this because students are not going to learn anything except a form of dependence. It is best to give a student a sense of methodology. The tutor should not approve or disapprove. He or she should teach them how to be self-critical, analytical and think about what their reaction is to the students work. The tutor should 'unpack' the work in front of the student and by doing so demonstrate or broaden the context in which they are working. *Graham Crowley (Royal College of Art)*

- Input from peers needs to be encouraged. If it's just the tutors talking and saying "this is right, this is wrong", then it's not going to work and students are not going to learn or come out of it happy. We need to make a learning environment that is cohesive so that they can develop. *Nathan Chenery (York St John University)*

- We decided to experiment this year in the drawing course by removing some one-to-one tutorials and replacing them with a seven-person crit. So seven people talking to each other about their work helps the other students' developing practice. *Kelly Chorpening (Camberwell College of Arts)*

- They have often come onto Foundation from a school situation where someone has told them that something is right or that something is wrong, or, what the 'correct' way of doing something is. If there is more than one member of staff in a crit, they may have opposing views about a piece of work and so students gradually understand that there will be a range of opinions and that ultimately they will have to make their own minds up about the direction of the work, informed by these opinions. *Sean Kaye (Leeds College of Art)*

- It's good to have two staff because it is often difficult to get students to have a healthy scepticism of what we say. They have come form a school world where the teacher's word is 'law'. I go to great lengths to tell the student that my word is not 'law' and that all they are getting is opinion. It's good for them to see the two members of staff arguing because they then have to decide whose voice to listen to. At the end of the day it's up to the student to take what they will from the different voices, and by that I mean not just the staff but also their contemporaries. That's something that the crit system does that no other system really puts in place. Suddenly there are all these opinions, and they are all relevant opinions, but maybe only one of them is any use to you. *Arthur Watson (Duncan of Jordanstone College of Art and Design)*

- We have done crits where staff leave the room and allow students to talk about work before coming back in and going through it. Another model is where we get a student to review another student's work so that the person presenting the work is not the student whose work it is. Rather, they talk to the student and they say, "Well this is what I think about it, would you agree? Is there anything else you would like to bring forward?" *Peter Day (University of Wolverhampton)*

- It's good for students to hear advice and criticism from the group but at the end of the day it's really important that they have their own integrity so that they maintain a real sense of what they want in the work and don't allow the advice from outside to force them into taking up positions that are not their own. *Alison Jones (Goldsmiths College)*

- How do you know what is that bit that you have got to hang on to? It's working out which bits can change but which bits are really you and are non-negotiable. That's part of the refining process that I think crits are very much about. It took me absolutely years to feel like I knew what I was doing when I was making work. But I remember when I got to that point then people stopped asking me "why did you do that?" and they just looked at it. That's when people started writing about it as well. It suddenly shifted and I realized I was in a different place. *Mark Dean (Goldsmiths College)*

PERCEPTIONS OF ASSESSMENT

Here the staff discuss student perceptions of assessment and how they endeavour to combat anxiety or any notions that staff judgement is influenced by personal taste:

- There is a direct relationship between crits, achievement, and feedback for students. They are useful for students to monitor progress, understand additional things that they may need to do or lines of enquiry relevant to their practice that they should pursue. From a staff perspective they allow us to review student progress and look at their work. Despite how relaxed you try to make them though, they are still very formal. Even if it's formative and not a final assessment, it's public and students don't want to be 'dissed' in front of other people. *Peter Day (University of Wolverhampton)*

- I think students are well aware that they are being assessed at some level. But think of it as CCTV. People don't think "Oh I'm on camera". I think we genuinely do think of it as this continual assessment. When people panic about it, " Oh my god it's my convenor", they freeze up which does not help them. *Mark Dean (Goldsmiths College)*

- In the crit we're talking about aesthetic judgement and there is fear that someone can make that judgement by virtue of their authority. *Roddy Hunter (York St John University)*

- There should be nothing to do with taste in art education. Here my role is to encourage and develop somebody else's work and so what I like has got nothing to do with it. In an educational environment working as an academic staff member, you are looking at a piece of work in the context of a larger body of work, which is an on-going progression over a course. It's not like going to a gallery. When I go to a gallery I become a member of the public that has chosen to go in because I have responded to the work. *Stuart MacKenzie (Glasgow School of Art)*

- One year we took our final year students to an exhibition every week. We also took our marking criteria, learning outcomes, and applied it to the professional work. It was hilarious because you'd go through it saying, "Well, this person is mega famous but I'm going to have to give this work a 2.2!" The students really enjoyed it and it showed them how we attempt to be objective in how we assess their work. It also gave them an idea of where those learning outcomes and marking criteria sit in the wider context so that they don't spend ages trying to figure them out and pass an exam as it were. We look at what their intention is as the starting point, and then how well they achieved that in terms of what materials they selected, what format they used, how well they researched what it is they're doing, and then finally, how well it has been resolved. *David Moore (Edinburgh College of Art)*

- Crits are often best when there's a lot of humour floating about as that means people are relaxed and don't feel as though they are being judged. I think the worst thing you can do to a discussion is formalize it at the beginning. If you put too many structures in place beforehand it becomes very stilted. I think it's important to reassure people as much as possible that there is very little at stake in a crit. One of the biggest obstacles in a crit is any sense of formality and the expectations that comes with it. The first time I do a crit with a group, I tend to start by making it really clear that I'm not assessing them. It's to reassure them that the process of evaluation is very low on the agenda and that critiques are an opportunity to share speculative viewpoints about the works. *Jim Hamlyn (Gray's School of Art)*

METHODS OF ASSESSMENT

Here staff give examples of some of the methods that can be used when assessing individual participation crits:

- There are summative and formative assessments. A summative assessment is where you bring in your work to the last crit, put it up and get graded on that. Formative crits happen throughout the year to give feedback and help you get to where you want to get with your work. Formative looks at the work leading up to the final piece, the knowledge gained, and the process – which is a huge part of what we do as creative people; we take that first idea, build it into something real, and refine it. That whole process is what most of our education is about in art, all those steps along the way. So you can't really take a piece of work, plonk it down at the end and then assess it because that doesn't take into account the research that has gone into it. So I feel that critiques can be a really valuable part of the formative assessment process. *Linda Lencovic (University of the Arts London)*

- The crits are assessed moments. The students that present in the crit are all part of a tutor group and that tutor will attend the crit along with one other member of staff as a way of broadening our assessment base. The ones that are presenting are the ones who are under scrutiny shall we say, by us. But we also take note of who is asking questions and who isn't. So at the end of term when we are assessing a student in our meetings, there is a general sense of participation. We also note how constructive their questions might be, how helpful, and whether they have really listened to what the person who is presenting is saying about their work. We look at whether they are asking what might be quite difficult questions because they are responding to the situation that they are presented, or whether they are just on their own hobby horse and causing a problem for other students. *Mark Dean (Goldsmiths College)*

- We introduced a pass/fail system of assessment in the first year. We moved away from graded assessment in order that the students could really start to learn how to work with different types of feedback. We felt that numerical grading was getting in the way of understanding feedback and understanding assessment. First year students also do an electronic journal where they write up their experiences of the crits and do a presentation on the feedback they've had from tutors and peers in order that they can see these different perspectives that they can draw on. *Roddy Hunter (York St John University)*

BARRIERS AND SOLUTIONS: TALKING ABOUT ART

In this chapter staff and industry professionals discuss some of the barriers that participants can face when talking about art. These include: a lack of confidence in reading art; having English as a second language; anxieties about public speaking; dyslexia; and dominance, silence or overuse of jargon by others in the group. They outline things that facilitators and other participants can do to support more confident and equal participation amongst all those in the group and give practical tips on the topic of reading art and speaking in public.

SILENCE

Silence amongst the audience can cause presenters to worry. Here the staff talk about why silence might occur, how it can be of benefit, and give strategies to help encourage participation where appropriate:

- Fear of speaking and expressing ideas in public is the biggest barrier, which can be overcome by asking questions that entice response and creating a relaxed atmosphere. *Angela Bartram (University of Lincoln)*

- The group is briefed at the beginning that people participate in different ways: someone may only say one thing over the three-week period that is really valuable and another might say something at every possible opportunity and not really be saying that much. Sometimes it's appropriate though for a group to say nothing for quite long periods of time. That's quite uncomfortable but it's the right thing as work is being done in that silence, thinking is being done. *Seán Cummins (Nottingham Trent University)*

- We often say at the beginning of a session that we'd like everyone to say at least one thing. We make it clear that there are no right or wrong things to say. *Joanne Lee (Nottingham Trent University)*

- You will have a couple of very confident people and others who are not and don't want to speak. All of the people in that situation will have ideas to contribute and the danger as a facilitator of a group like that is if you let the confident people take over. If you do others will disengage and if they are constantly not contributing they will start to disengage from that process altogether. A lot of people don't want to speak and even though it's tough for a number of reasons, the best thing to do is to tell them that you will be picking on them and force them to say something. The motivations behind why people study, have difficulties or engage in certain types of behaviour are incredibly important because they are changeable and exposable. So if you care, if you are bothered about why someone sits quietly in a corner and does not do something, and if you want to make opportunities for them to blossom, it's rare that they won't take those up. It's rare that they won't then change and become a more engaged student. *Katie Streten (Imagination)*

- I remember sitting in on a seminar group that was being run by one of the best colleagues I ever worked with. It was one of those situations where no one was going to talk. He put a big smile on his face, folded his arms, and sat there for five whole minutes until one of them cracked. Anyone else would have started babbling to fill the silence, but he said, "No, this is your seminar, you lead it". Fabulous! A good crit is where everybody says something. Even if it's just a little voice from the back, at least that person will have crossed that boundary of giving an opinion no matter how slight it is. Once they do that they are in the room. It's a building thing. *Arthur Watson (Duncan of Jordanstone College of Art and Design)*

- I remember as a student being asked to speak and feeling sometimes that it was a bit forced or that I did not have enough time to reflect on things. The good thing about asking people things is that it keeps them awake. There is this other method called 'pounce and bounce' where you pounce on someone and then randomly you bounce it off someone else. So they say something, and then you ask someone else, "well, what do you think?" and they might have a different perspective. However, as with all formulae, the more you do it, the more people cotton onto it being a formula and they work out strategies for avoiding being asked, or for getting around the question. So I think it's good to try a number of different strategies instead of homing in on one. *Jim Hamlyn (Gray's School of Art)*

- We have an online blog that students can use to give and receive critique of their work before the crit and it also takes staff out of the equation. Feedback on the blog tends to be a bit more considered as people have time to reflect on it before they post and they have had time to look at the work in a bit more detail first too so have warmed up. They might also use a different language that they are more comfortable with than they would at the crit. The presenter also has then already had someone give them feedback and so they can talk through what criticism they have already received. Saying that, there were issues. The students that did not get a great deal of commentary wondered why people were not commenting on their work. *Peter Day (University of Wolverhampton)*

- When I do a crit I always start by asking everyone to walk around and look at all of the work. It's so they familiarise themselves with the work and prepare questions but it's also so we can make cross-references later on and we don't have to go from left to right with ten minutes each. It keeps people on their toes! *Roddy Hunter (York St John University)*

- It's important to make the audience really think about the kinds of questions that they are going to ask and maybe do some preparatory work on these. It's good to get them to develop a repertoire of questions or comments that can help that other person develop their practice. Making the time to think about that interaction is really important and it's important to make sure they understand that their participation is incredibly important to someone else's learning. *Alison James (London College of Fashion)*

DOMINANCE

Sometimes individual staff or students can dominate the discussion, which can prevent others in the group from having an input. The staff discuss this issue:

STAFF DOMINANCE:

- Staff can dominate because they are uneasy about silence but they should resist. What I love about art is that it embraces all kinds of interpretations and as a teacher I think it's our role to encourage other people's creation and not our own. The more I teach the more I realize that actually being invisible is probably the best thing that you can do. I don't mean that you should extract yourself from the teaching but more that some of the best teaching is where you are creating a situation for people to discover for themselves what they learn. Then because they feel that they are doing it themselves they take ownership of it. *Jim Hamlyn (Gray's School of Art)*

- My greatest worry in crits is when I realize that most of the conversation has been from the tutors. I have, on occasion, heard myself and colleagues holding court on hobby-horse topics, and I know it is surely a delusion to think that students do not also recognize this when this is happening. Student engagement in the process is essential, and tutors must listen to what is being said by them. *Robert Armstrong (National College of Art and Design)*

- As a staff team, we have had quite complex conversations about what we think ought to go on in those sessions and how best to facilitate discussion, which means that the staff try not to speak a great deal or lead the conversation. Quite consciously we are trying to say that all of us are equally present in the room and that what each person has to say is relevant. *Seán Cummins (Nottingham Trent University)*

STUDENT DOMINANCE:

- A bad crit is one where it becomes a performance for the staff or a particularly egotistical student to take centre stage and not actually let anyone else get a word in edgeways. It becomes more about the performance than it does about the work. In a cohort of students you are always going to have the people that are good at talking the talk but not walking the walk. And you get people who cannot talk at all, but do walk the walk. That's how things are in life and you are dealing with life all the time. Good teaching is being aware of that spectrum and not being too loose or too tight. *Bernadette Blair (Kingston University)*

- You can get into to this thing called 'master readings', where someone, not necessarily the teacher, interprets the work to such a high degree that for everyone else there seems nothing left to say. They are left to pick morsels off a bone that has been stripped. That also leads to the idea that there is some kind of definitive interpretation that trumps all others – but I don't think that's the case. *Jim Hamlyn (Gray's School of Art)*

- You are going to get very strong, or at least very vocal students who will want to say everything and think they have all the answers. So it's how you balance allowing them to say enough but not too much that it destabilizes the whole conversation and how you do it without them feeling that they have been cut off! *Alistair Payne (Glasgow School of Art)*

LANGUAGE

Language can be a barrier to participation in crits in all sorts of ways. Here staff talk about the difficulties that can be caused by overuse of jargon, specialist or even vague language, and uncontextualised references by some in the group. They also discuss ways that those who have English as a second language might also find it challenging and suggest ways to support participation:

THE ANXIETY CAUSED THROUGH USE OF JARGON AND SPECIALIST LANGUAGE:

- Sometimes when students are talking about work or writing their academic essays, they think that they have to adopt a certain kind of voice; that they need to sound academic for example. But it's important to speak in plain English so everyone understands it. *Alison James (London College of Fashion)*

- Tutors and students should speak in plain English so that everyone can grasp the nub of the issue. It takes great effort, intelligence and application to address complex, subtle and sophisticated ideas and thoughts in a language that can easily be understood. *Graham Crowley (Royal College of Art)*

- When I facilitate sessions I am often not versed on that particular sector. That's often beneficial as I don't know the jargon or the acronyms and so I am using pretty straightforward language. If I don't understand something I ask the person speaking to explain it to me, and that is good for other people in the room who also maybe don't know but feel more embarrassed about asking the question. *Alison Coward (Bracket)*

- Students are regularly required to write statements on their work and workshops are conducted where the use of jargon will be contested in favour of clarity to help them to consider and develop the work. There is nothing worse than listening to ill-digested Lacan being regurgitated in a crit. It is a benefit of holding discussions in studio that talk can be brought back to practical matters about material and how exactly things are 'working' or not. *Robert Armstrong (National College of Art and Design)*

UNCONTEXTUALISED REFERENCES:

- Sometimes there are specificities of language that the students may encounter when doing their own research. If they are working in photography, they might be reading about photographic theory and looking at photographic practice. Then in crits they encounter a set of debates that other students on the course, who are perhaps making sculpture, are immersed in. The crit might bring people together that don't all speak the same language and so the conversation is operating on lots of different levels. When they go out into the world as practitioners, they are going to have to convey what it is that are doing to multiple audiences, whether it's a curator, funder, whoever, and it's important that that can communicate to people. It's important to say, "Oh did you hear that word? That's quite a particular word" and exploring it. If someone uses the word 'punctum' in a photography sense, then all of the painters and sculptors may be thinking, "What's that?" It's important to reveal those terms and make people aware of what is being said. *Joanne Lee (Nottingham Trent University)*

- I think it is a matter of etiquette when anybody introduces a name, whether it's Wittgenstien, Plato or Elizabeth Taylor, they should contextualize and explain who that person is. This is because there's always someone in the room that comes from another cultural background, where people like Elizabeth Taylor are not well known. *Graham Crowley (Royal College of Art)*

VAGUENESS OF LANGUAGE:

- We end seminars by asking the presenter whether the crit was useful and if there is anything else they would like to ask the group. We try to ensure that the vague terms that get used like 'nice' or 'I like it' can be substantiated into something that a student can use. *Bernadette Blair (Kingston University)*

- I think the word 'nice' should be obliterated from teachers and students vocabulary. It's such a grey word. What does it actually mean? It can be interpreted as being quite insulting if your work is nice. I think there needs to be a gloves off discussion about subjectivity with students. I think students need to understand that in a critical arena, anything can be said, provided it can be substantiated and it is not emotionally based. *Ann Hulland (Kingston University)*

- As an artist I'm interested to know whether this bit works, or that bit works, not whether people like or don't like it. *Stuart MacKenzie (Glasgow School of Art)*

- Students that are new to the process will immediately jump to judgement without even realizing that they are doing it i.e. "I like that" or "that's good". They skip the description of what it is and any interpretation of what it is trying to do as though they know these other things. You have to pull them back and say, "lets find out *what* is actually 'good' about it". *Jim Hamlyn (Gray's School of Art)*

- We ask students to describe what they respond to within the work, what is it that they consider to be engaging, which elements they consider to be less successful. This forces students to think about successful and unsuccessful elements within a work rather than just allowing them to say, "I like it" or "I don't like it". *Sean Kaye (Leeds College of Art)*

STUDENTS THAT HAVE ENGLISH AS A SECOND LANGUAGE:

- If you are facilitating a crit with maybe ten students, each of those students is a different individual. There are potentially enormous cultural and social differences just in that group and if you take five out and put another five in, the whole dynamic has changed. You have got to be very aware of that dynamic. Sometimes international students that come in might have had a really different experience in the country that they have studied in previously. They might not have had crits in the institution that they have come from and it's a radical thing for them to actually engage with other students in that environment. You have got to be prepared and aware of those differences. That's where good facilitation comes in and where it's down to the staff member to support those students. Maybe those students start by just listening. You allow them gradually to work into the dynamic, to understand that there is a discussion taking place, and how they fit within this environment that is being constructed for them. Crits are good things and you just have to find your place in them. *Alistair Payne (Glasgow School of Art)*

- It's really difficult for some of our international students who have to present their ideas in a public forum in another language. And it's not just that, it's also negotiating specialist subject vocabulary, social interjects, fielding questions from the floor, maybe not always being very clear about what they have heard or what people are saying. There are a lot of challenges. *Alison James (London College of Fashion)*

- It's really hard for the students talking and for those listening and trying really hard to understand when we have students whose English is really poor. I encourage them to go to English class and work really hard because unless their language develops they are really not going to get everything that they can out of the Goldsmiths type of teaching and learning because it's so discursive. *Alison Jones (Goldsmiths College)*

- You must be patient. You must not vocalize for someone else what it is they are thinking. You must wait for someone to find the words that they want to use. You could say, "do you mean this?" but that's going to be terrible for someone's confidence if you are suggesting that you know what they are thinking. So you do need to be patient, slow things down, and switch the attention if need be. *Roddy Hunter (York St John University)*

- There are two issues. One is English as a second language and the other is a broader cultural language. In some cultures it's more acceptable to assert yourself in public than others. There are also different attitudes towards materials and how things are made. There are also different political and cultural references that people have. In the past few years though, students who used to be quieter in convenors, asking "Is what I'm interested in culturally relevant? Does it fit? Do I fit in here?" and who might have come through the extension degree, are now leading the way, in bringing their own experience into a convenor and tutorial situation. *Mark Dean (Goldsmiths College)*

- I think there definitely needs to be awareness of what culture and what interaction culture people are bringing with them. Usually we think of Scandinavians as not having a problem because their English is very good usually, but they have a culture where you are not critical of other people and that could affect how they interact. The way I have done it is by making the whole group aware of each other's backgrounds by having some sort of introduction where students actually talk about the way things are done in their own country or in their previous education. Sometimes English students can get a little bit frustrated when students can't always get out what they mean either because of shyness or because of the quality of their language. But it's a question of being patient, and supporting people to feel that they are in an environment that is helpful. *Bernadette Blair (Kingston University)*

- We run Erasmus and it's great to have an international mix of students, not for cynical reasons like the extra finance, but for educational reasons. An international class means that all students really are in a world arena with their practice, and the more they can understand the perceptions of other cultures and the way that art is considered and taught in other cultures, the better. *Ann Hulland (Kingston University)*

- We are operating in a global learning environment and that means that different students can have very different ways of looking at and judging work. There are similarities, but even the idea of how or whether you talk about work, whether you can be critical or not critical, can be very much a part of your academic or social culture. I think that is something that needs to be addressed because if you sit a group of people down that are from different parts of the world and ask them to follow one rule, then they need to know what that rule is! So explicit ground rules in crits are crucial. *Linda Lencovic (University of the Arts London)*

FINDING THE 'RIGHT' LANGUAGE:

- When you are a student you might start changing the way that you speak, and using new words that you pick up on, which is all a good thing. You start picking up on how other people criticize work using new vocabularies but sometimes that can overwhelm your own language and one of the most important things when speaking is that you make yourself clear and known. If you start using other people's words, that will disappear. I try to encourage simplicity as far as possible. *Katie Streten (Imagination)*

- •In the early years it is inevitable that students will start to mirror the tutor. They hear a kind of 'art speak' and start talking that way in the belief that this is the only way to talk about art. That's one way of learning and developing the language for your discipline, but I think it takes a long time to develop your own language and part of that process is developing confidence in your own 'voice' as an artist. *Linda Lencovic (University of the Arts London)*

- Operate within the parameters of your discipline but be authentic, be you, and have your own voice. *Alison James (London College of Fashion)*

- There are ways that you can develop the language to talk about things, especially things that are unnameable. One of the things that we encourage them to do is get involved with creative writing because it helps them string thoughts together and open them off into different territories. We get them to read as much as possible. We also get then to think about how art itself is articulated. So for instance with the first years, we took them away and each evening they were shown different films about art and artists. There was a film on Basquiat, an old film about Michelangelo, a film on Pollock. We were asking them how people are articulating the practice of being an artist in these played-out roles. One of things we are trying to get them to think about is how you play out the role of being an artist. So then when you are presenting it's not you saying all this but you a, dramatic persona of yourself as an artist. It gives a bit of space. *Garry Barker (Leeds College of Art)*

INTERPRETING ART

'Reading' an artwork can be difficult; particularly if it's something you've not been shown how to do before. In this section staff talk about some of the difficulties that students can face when interpreting an art work and present some strategies that can help people find a 'way in'.

LEARNING TO LOOK:

- Everyone is so accustomed to looking at images on screen that if you are not careful you make a facsimile of an artwork and not an art work. It's an idea of an artwork but it's not been invested in in terms of materials, techniques, finish, etc. to become something more, something visually arresting. *Kelly Chorpening (Camberwell College of Arts)*

- Learning to look and process what we are seeing is important. There is so much stuff out there that students can jump to a kind of "Oh, I could do one of those", forgetting that they need to process it before they get to that point. *Miraj Ahmed (Architectural Association/ Cambridge University)*

- When we ask students to write about their work, they tend to leap frog over the materials, the visual properties, even how the work of art has been made and go straight to the ideas and theories. Last year I did a matching game, where I had artist's writings about work and the visuals – but not together – and I asked people to match written statement to artwork. Usually the guesses were way off what the person had written. Last week we were having a crit and everyone was getting into clever language and I kept saying that what we are looking at here is a circle on a piece of paper. I was trying to bring it back to the actual formal presence of what it is that's in front of us: "Here is an A2 piece of black paper with a large circle drawn in white pencil", not necessarily a "signifier of existential angst". You can't skip a work's visual qualities because ultimately, that's what you're left with. *Kelly Chorpening (Camberwell College of Arts)*

LAYERS OF INTERPRETATION:

- The term "visual literacy" is one I find difficult. I understand where it comes from but I have a problem with the term because it suggests that there is a dictionary that you can go to, to find out the meanings of things – and visual images don't really work like that. Obviously there are a whole set of codes, references, associations, metaphors, styles and genres and they are all things that inform the meaning of images, but they are vague and contested. You can also do things like a feminist reading, a Marxist reading, a psychoanalytical reading. You can do that with one work and come up with so many different and equally plausible interpretations. *Jim Hamlyn (Gray's School of Art)*

FINDING A WAY IN – STRATEGIES FOR READING AN IMAGE:

- I like to spend the first 10 minutes before we start, walking around with the students and taking notes, paying attention to: "What it is that comes to mind when you are looking at this?" "Are you noticing how it's made?" "Are you thinking about what it signifies?" "Is there something getting in the way?" I also quite like to ask three questions: "What's fundamental?" "What's underdeveloped?" "What's superfluous?" As they've already walked around we can then make cross-references later on. We can make a decision to compare one artist's use of particular medium to another artist's use of the same medium if that's where the flow goes. Usually there is a point where it seems natural to go from one artist's work to another, because we have all looked at it together, and we are all aware of the work that is coming up to look at next. *Roddy Hunter (York St John University)*

- When we ask students to talk about another student's work we encourage them to begin by stating the obvious. We ask. "What are we looking at?" "Is this a painting on canvas, or is it an object?" "What is this object made of?" By starting to state the obvious they can then build associations. We then ask, "What does it remind you of, does it relate to other things?" Hopefully by starting here, making a contribution in a crit is not too threatening as the students are not being asked to say what something means, they are simply being asked to describe what they are looking at. This approach does two things: it aids an understanding of visual literacy and analysing work, and it allows students to gain confidence in speaking in public situations. Gradually students grow in confidence in relation to talking about art work. *Sean Kaye (Leeds College of Art)*

- At the early stages I ask students to describe things that they see as though someone is listening to them on the radio. There is always a tendency to jump to the subject matter or content and sometimes that can be a jump too far. It's good to start critiques with the most basic things. I think sometimes students feel that that's a bit too rudimentary and they launch straight into interpretation, which can be fine, but I find that simple descriptions are immensely generative. This is simply because people describe things differently. If you get one student to describe something and you get another to describe the same thing, the descriptions will be quite different. It shows you that there is interpretation going on from the very beginning and they can recognise that there are interpretations and insights that they are having about things that they might not even be aware of, and that those have value that they are not aware of. The other thing I suppose that is really vital is that children are very good at critique, and coming up with novel interpretations that can often be really good, and are often quite unselfconscious. Sometimes it's the self-consciousness that can be difficult for people. *Jim Hamlyn (Gray's School of Art)*

× To begin with we are really only talking about very simple things, like: What are we actually looking at? What does it look like? What does it remind you of? The tutors can keep expanding on things to open up conversations about contemporary art practice, about the use of materials, and about the use of vocabulary that you would use to describe work. They might be quite inventive and expansive in the way that they do that and talk about work even in terms of gestures or sounds. For example, "That looks a little bit 'pop!' " It surprises the students and they are like, "Wow, what does he mean by that?!" It loosens them up a bit, and gets them used to the idea of talking all the time. Another way that we encourage participation is to find ways of discussing work that are easy to begin with. For instance, I'll go to a gallery with them ask them to pick a work that they either find interesting, have something that they want to say about it, or something they find completely puzzling and so they have a question for the rest of the group. In doing that it doesn't matter whether or not they like something, want to talk about it, or feel completely baffled by it, they have a road into the crit. It's about getting people started. I always say that you don't have to say anything complicated. You might just say "I like it because it's blue" and then we discuss that and what that means. It's finding a way for them to cross that first hurdle that's really important. *David Moore (Edinburgh College of Art)*

× I have a document here that contains possible questions that could come up in a crit. We put this together as a staff group. We sat around a table and just listed what a crit is and what might come up in a crit.

Point 1. Picture structure, composition, construction, design; Point 2. Content, what is the subject matter of the work – not just the pictured objects; Point 3. How well has the work been physically produced and the idea made clear in visual form? Point 4. Concept, What is the idea, thought, feeling, activity, that prompted the picture? How does it work, if it does, why doesn't it if not? Point 5. Context, What is the context in which this work resides in terms of visual art, historical and contemporary art, and the wider world we live in? *Stuart MacKenzie (Glasgow School of Art)*

× We start the analysis of visual literacy with an awareness of the body. In terms of theory we introduce phenomenology, existentialism and the idea of the embodied mind. One of the reasons for that is that we can start conceptual thinking on the twinned realities of the body and making. For instance, say someone is making a painting: Is it vertical? Is it horizontal? Is it like you standing vertically? Is it bilaterally symmetrical? Is it in balance? Is it like you standing on one leg? We do lots of stuff in crits where everyone gets physically and actively involved. I stand students in front of work and say, "Can we mime how this is made?" So if it's a painting, are the marks going like this? …

(He gestures)

…Immediately there is a language of the body. From that we look at where the language of the words comes from. This is where playing comes in. We start with words that come from the body, like "We have grasped this concept", "I have digested this information" "I think this is in balance". So they have a sense that their whole body is part of their understanding and that's an interesting thing for an artist to take on board. As we make something, we are telling a story of the relationship with the world out there, through the material we use and the way we use it. So it starts with a bodily understanding and from that it's a lot easier to develop concepts and words that try to explain what it is that they are trying to do. So by having the mind embodied in that way it gives us an approach into this internal world. Students will often be unable to articulate what they are trying to do because they have not yet linked the internal mind to the external reality. So we start at this level and then as they develop intellectual concepts, we look at where the intellectual concept is rooted in the knowing of the body. *Garry Barker (Leeds College of Art)*

- You read art from a set of experiences and those almost endless set of references embedded in your skull. You also read it in terms of the sensuous pleasure it gives you. Both of those are totally subjective. What might be amazing to you might be absolutely disgusting to someone else. You're also trying to work out what the idea behind this it is or might be, what the mind-set of the person who did this is, what they are trying to achieve, what it is saying to you, how it reflects what they know about art, what it reflects about stuff they have never seen but would be amazed to see. There are so many different things and every student and every piece of work we are approaching with a different tack. *Arthur Watson (Duncan of Jordanstone College of Art and Design)*

- A parallel process to the crit occurs in final year BA whereby students at an early meeting agree a number of thematic areas of common interest. I will try to group these themes into a series of seminars, which focus on the suggested topics as a basis for fortnightly seminars to which students contribute images, video links or texts, (not their own work) which they introduce to the assembled group. Discussion centres on the themes without direct discussion or presentation of the students' own work. These seminars work well in opening up discussion about the 'reading' of work by other artists. The alternating and parallel individual presentations benefit from the objectivity fostered in the thematic seminars. *Robert Armstrong (National College of Art and Design)*

PUBLIC SPEAKING

A fear of speaking in public can affect both those who are presenting and those who are part of the audience. However, public speaking is an essential component of the crit and there are also many other situations in life where public speaking is needed. Below, the staff and industry professionals give practical tips about how people can gain confidence when speaking in front of a group.

INTRODUCING PEOPLE TO PUBLIC SPEAKING:

- There are so many times as a creative student and as a professional in the creative industries that you need to speak, whether it's in class, in a crit, in meetings, or when pitching for business. There are so many scenarios and you need to feel OK about doing it. It's very easy to think 'oh I won't participate', 'I won't speak' or 'I won't do that meeting', but the people that do, tend to get ahead. *Laura North (Speaking Out)*

- I think we assume that by the time people get to university, especially if they are mature students, that they have enough life experience that they will know how to do these things. I think we rely on the fact that someone else will teach them somewhere. I think the other thing that comes into the equation is that sometimes people in art schools are a little bit suspicious of anything that smacks of corporate or a bit too polished. *Alison James (London College of Fashion)*

- A way of easing people in is to break people into groups, get them to work with and then present to each other one to one, then to the group, and then to the larger group. That makes them realise that presenting is not too scary and gives them opportunity to practice. The more you do it, the more relaxed you feel about it. *Laura North (Speaking Out)*

CALMING NERVES:

- I think the first thing is that anyone who tells you they are not nervous when they are doing public speaking is either lying or incredibly unusual. Most people have a certain level of nerves when it comes to speaking in public and so when you're nervous it's important to remind people that everyone is in the same boat. *Katie Streten (Imagination)*

- There are some things that are hard to manage like if you suddenly flush and go pink from top to toe. The only way you can manage that is to just accept it's going to happen, breath and be calm. A very simple technique that I have learned from a number of people over the years is to breathe in slowly through your nose for a count of five, and then out through your mouth for a count of eleven. Also find some space beforehand, chill out and get in control. Think about where the tension is: Is it in my neck? Try to relax my shoulders, how I am standing, have I got all my limbs crossed over, can I stand and open up my posture in a way that will enable me to breath a bit better? Are my feet planted on the floor? Think about the body and just loosening it up. That's a very good technique for releasing tension. *Alison James (London College of Fashion)*

- There are ways to stand to feel more grounded, like putting your feet straight down into the ground and leaning forward slightly so that you are not rocking too much. And little psychological things like smiling when you first start speaking or saying hello to your audience because it relaxes you and breaks down that rather scary gulf between yourself and the audience. *Katie Streten (Imagination)*

- Neuro-linguistic programming has a whole raft of techniques for dealing with either things that trigger nerves or trying to get over particularly difficult patterns. We are often nervous because we have had a bad experience and we rehearse that bad experience. So any techniques that are going to help you get rid of you replaying that terrible time in your head. Visualization is a really good technique and instead of rehearsing "Oh my god wouldn't it be awful if I fluffed or dropped things", in visualization you think about what is the best possible outcome and you imagine it. You imagine it in such a real way that you can imagine the temperature of the room, the gaze of the people, how you are feeling inside, how your material is coming across, and you conjure in your head this picture of success. It may sound a bit funny but elite sports people do it all the time. It's that psychological management that you are doing to get in control of your mind and your nerves. And it's amazing how you can trick yourself into visualizing that outcome and actually managing to produce it in some way. *Alison James (London College of Fashion)*

- Look at your smilers and nodders because if you are up there and you can see a smiler or a nodder, then instantly you have got someone who is a friendly face in the room. If you haven't got any, or you are too nervous to make specific eye contact, look at a point just above their heads. *Alison James (London College of Fashion)*

PREPARE:

- If you have a presentation that is well structured, rehearsed and you know exactly where you are going with it, you are less likely to panic about leaving stuff out or giving the wrong answer to questions. That gives you a base level of confidence before you even start speaking. Write out what you are going to say, summarize that and put it into a format whereby if you lose your place in the middle of a speech you can pick it up again quite easily. Make notes on succinct cards but do not learn your speech off by heart because if someone interrupts you, you will get thrown. Also, speak slowly. Other ways to prepare are to film yourself and look at the little ticks and strange things that everyone does with their voice, hands or body when they speak – and deal with those before you even get into a speaking situation. *Katie Streten (Imagination)*

- Think what the worst possible question that you could get asked is and write your answer down. Do that for others you think of. That does one of two things: one, if the question comes up you have a ready answer for it but it also picks out flaws in what you have put together. So you shouldn't get into that situation anyway. *Katie Streten (Imagination)*

- There are what are known as hygiene factors. You want to know that your power point will work, that your model will stand up right, that your team knows where to come in when you are doing a group presentation. *Alison James (London College of Fashion)*

- I let students practice by making a one-minute presentation on something that they are interested in and knowledgeable about. You then take that one minute and make it five minutes. Roddy *Hunter (York St John University)*

- If you have a specific learning difficulty like dyslexia, you might find the actual preparation, organising or scripting of your presentation a bit hard. Features of dyslexia are very varied however, and many that have it can actually be incredibly articulate, fabulous speakers. If you ask someone with dyslexia to tell you about their practice they will often be really rich in ideas in a way that maybe someone who does not have any problem in terms of structuring and organizing it might not. So there are benefits and challenges. *Alison James (London College of Fashion)*

- As an audience member you can also prepare questions that you want to ask. *Katie Streten (Imagination)*

GETTING YOUR MESSAGE ACROSS:

- Think about what are your three key messages? What are the three most important things you want people to remember from what you are going to talk about? Ask yourself where your message might wane, where you might lose them, and how you can talk so as not to lose them at critical moments. *Alison James (London College of Fashion)*

- Being heard is important. If you have a quiet voice and on top of that you are nervous, how do you get over that? A lot comes down to how you stand. Your body is a sound box and so the more relaxed your body is, the more relaxed you feel, the bigger and brighter the sound will be that comes out of you. So the whole thing about standing slightly forward, and in a relaxed position helps people to speak more loudly. Some of the students understand singing techniques, so I talk about that with them because it's all about using the diaphragm area as well. *Katie Streten (Imagination)*

BODY LANGUAGE:

- Body language is incredibly important when you are presenting. There are three ways of using body language: If you are a very animated person and you speak a lot with your hands waving high in the air, there is a lot of emphasis going on, and you immediately start to cause tension, anxiety, and it all feels a bit hectic. On the other hand, if you stand with your hands by your side or in your pockets and don't move, there is an instant withdrawal and removal from the audience and that's not a good thing. So what you want is for your hands to move in the central plane of your body. That actually makes other people feel relaxed. So if you find that you are the kind of person that grips your notes or wants to put your hands in your pocket, or fold your arms, the easiest thing to do, and it will feel very strange, is to take your notes, anchor your elbows into your waist and practice moving your forearms in and our as you speak (see video). When you practice it you will feel like an idiot! But the net effect is that you will get used to having your hands in the right space, you will start to move them in a slightly more fluid way, gradually your elbows start to come out from your side, and you get to a more comfortable space. But it means that you are not rigid, not manic, like this, and it makes you and your audience more relaxed. *Katie Streten (Imagination)*

- The presentational mechanics can often get overlooked because people see them as secondary to the delivery of the content. But it's amazing how many lost opportunities there are because people don't understand about how to make eye contact with the group, how to work a room, how to make sure that you are talking to everybody, how to make sure that your voice can be heard at the back, how to project a confident and engaging persona even if you are really not feeling it inside. I have sat through a number of sessions where either people have not made eye contact and it's felt like some kind of alien monologue, or someone has started off by saying something really interesting but then their voice just trails away because they have not understood the simple tip of keeping your voice up, level, and alive when you are talking to someone. As a result that key point that they are making at the end can often disappear. As an audience member you get a bit irritated. You feel frustrated because you want to say "No, speak up, I actually want to hear what you have to say, I am interested, but you are trailing off and I am missing half of what you want me to get and it's affecting my willingness to engage". It's about the facilitation of your message. You want people to get what you are about and if you can talk to people, they can understand. If they feel you are with them in the room and you are genuinely into what you are talking about, genuinely passionate about your work and your subject, I think that makes up for an awful lot. *Alison James (London College of Fashion)*

BE YOURSELF:

- I think my number one tip is to believe in your subject. If you are interested, keen, have researched it, and are thinking about your position in relation to it, then even if the rest of your presentation has raw edges, that belief, that interest and passion, will come through. *Alison James (London College of Fashion)*

- Think about how to maintain momentum. It's almost better to do less, but do it in your style for the maximum impact. I don't mean dancing on tables, your impact might be a very gentle, calm kind of delivery. Just think about how to keep their attention and interest. *Alison James (London College of Fashion)*

- Remember that you are not talking *at* somebody; this is a conversation. Even if they say less than you do, it is an interaction, and just remembering that is paramount. *Alison James (London College of Fashion)*

- It can be hard for those who have English as a second language. Their written work might be really good but they may not feel so confident with their speaking and so they want to use their written work as a comfort blanket because they know that what they have written is correct. But reading your words is bad for a number of reasons. It means there is no rapport with your audience because you are not looking at them, it means that if something happens and you lose your place you have to go through the text to find out where you were before, and it also removes that element of spontaneity and humanity that is there is the best speakers. *Katie Streten (Imagination)*

MANAGING FEEDBACK FROM THE GROUP:

- Other people like to make a statement rather than ask a question. If that's contrary to what you've said and you're not sure how to respond, just say, "Thank you so much what a very interesting point" and move on. *Katie Streten (Imagination)*

- If you have points to make but can't get them across because people are interrupting, just say "I'm sorry, I'll answer that at the end", or, would you mind if I finish this before we answer your question? *Katie Streten (Imagination)*

- If you are asked a question you don't understand, the best thing to say is, "I don't understand your question, could you please rephrase it?" Very often the problem is not with you. I always make the point to the students that if someone asks you a question, it is their responsibility to ask it in say that can be understood. If that doesn't work the best thing to do then is ask if they can write it down and say that you'll take it away and find out for them after the meeting. It takes the pressure off, means that you don't have to deal with it then, but it does mean that you will still genuinely answer that question. *Katie Streten (Imagination)*

- A Dictaphone is useful because what's been said and what's been heard may not always be the same thing. *Alison James (London College of Fashion)*

- We have a student note taker so that the student presenting does not have to try and remember, think, and talk all at the same time and so that the conversation that's happening is actually a conversation. *Ann Hulland (Kingston University)*

HOW THINGS HAVE CHANGED: STAFF REFLECT ON THEIR OWN CRITS

In this chapter the staff reflect back on what their own crits were like and how they differ from or influence the models they use today:

- I went to art school in the 1970s and did not have crits or tutorials. I had a few seminars and lectures in the first year and that was it. I was in the studio, the staff were in the studio, I watched them, they watched me, and we made work. It was building tacit knowledge. We could ask questions but you tended to watch and then do and that was how you learned. There was not a lot of conversation that went on but there was a lot of reflection. Reflective practice through doing, that seemed to be what my five years were about. That all changed though when art schools became polytechnics and polytechnics became universities as it's very hard to justify that type of education. I don't even know what I got. I think I passed! But it did not seem that important because I was not there to get a degree I suppose. *Richard Bell (University of Leeds)*

- Going back to the mid 1970s when I was at college, there were no formal, timetabled crits, just informal discussions in the pub. Tutors were often there but it was not formalized in terms of a room and a work; that just did not happen. *Jim Birrell (Glasgow School of Art)*

- It was more about the atelier. The older staff members would have their own space, they would very much focus on their own careers as artists, and they would come in from time to time. Culturally it was a different time. *Stuart MacKenzie (Glasgow School of Art)*

- Tutors would not necessarily have anything to say but they would want to leave you with the impression that they are intelligent, thoughtful people. So they would say, "Your work is interesting" and you'd think, "Oh my work is interesting". *Graham Crowley (Royal College of Art)*

- Nobody had crits in art school. The word 'idea' was rarely heard in the early years, the old Diploma course was very much about skill-based training. It was very different. In fourth year people might start asking about ideas because it was a little more self-motivated, but no crits, that was a new one. *Arthur Watson (Duncan of Jordanstone College of Art and Design)*

- As students we would finish working for the day and then go to the pub. We would talk about art and that would be where we had the debate, and often quite a heated debate as well! Back in those days the staff used to join and it was a lot more informal. So in a sense that was my experience of the crit. It is the bad experiences that have helped me think about what needs to take place in a crit, and how I establish that and work with students in that environment. *Alistair Payne (Glasgow School of Art)*

- The crits I had as a student tended to be the Michael Asher[3] kind. They were extremely long and led by an American who tended to talk a lot. He spoke fascinatingly it has to be said, and captivatingly, but then again there's a difference between being captivated by something and participating. *Jim Hamlyn (Gray's School of Art)*

- For some people there was a real sense of disempowerment within the process, particularly as a result of the male lecturers. When I interviewed people for a study on the topic, many suggested that it was more of an ego trip for a lot of lecturers and that the students presenting did not seem to be important. The consensus I got was that the platform was the lecturer's and the students were really only presenting work to

3. An artist and professor known for the lengthy crits, of up to 12 hours, that he used to run on his Post-Studio course at the California Institute of Arts.

allow lecturers to say whatever they wanted about whatever theory they were interested in at the time! Students don't really have a role in that situation, and that's not what a crit is about. *Peter Day (University of Wolverhampton)*

- Many people say that it was like pulling teeth. They did not want to open their mouths to say anything and that's of no value to anyone. What learning is going on in an environment where a student is pre-occupied with the fear of what's going on or what's going to happen to them?! *Bernadette Blair (Kingston University)*

- I did my BA in Canada and my MA here at Chelsea. Although completely different countries, they have very similar ways of dealing with crits. You knew what time you were supposed to show up, you brought your work, sat down and people were supposed to talk about the work. There weren't really any ground rules or structure set out. It was something that was being done *to* you. You almost felt that it was for someone else's benefit, not your own. *Linda Lencovic (University of the Arts London)*

- I learned that you have to find your own way and do what you need to do and that if someone does not like what do you do then that's their problem, not yours. Also, crits shouldn't be about personal taste. I used to get brought into universities and art colleges in the 80s, especially in a school where there were black students an all white male staff. I remember talking to a young black woman who did paintings of her grandmother and the lecturers did not get it at all. They were asking her why she was painting old ugly people. Her paintings were stunning, full of love, the colours were amazing, shape and form was exciting, but the lecturers could not get past the surface. That's a problem in critiques if you have someone that cannot relate to your work at all and if they can't see past their own prejudice. *Rita Keegan (Artist)*

× I was a student at NCAD in the early 70's, at a time of great unrest – post '68, the 'troubles in Northern Ireland', and revolt in art education in Ireland. My generation of art students received almost no education in art, but quite a lot in social agitation and politics. When I commenced as a student the college was directly controlled by the Department of Education, staffed by members of the Royal Hibernian Academy, and the staff imposed a regime of drawing from life and plaster casts in a very reactionary environment. Skill was everything! My time there coincided with the overthrow of that structure and the establishment of an independent autonomous college. During this time the college was closed on a number of occasions and I was twice expelled for 'insubordination'! The closest we got to having crits was student meetings to plan occupying the college and setting up alternative spaces. I am all too aware of parallels at present as NCAD moves towards a merger with UCD [University College Dublin]. I worry that the independence fought for long ago will be lost in the University, but arguments against this are difficult in the current economic climate and drive towards mergers of every kind. *Robert Armstrong (National College of Art and Design)*

× I think crits have changed. When I was a student they were pretty tough and quite brutal in the sense that it was very direct, there was no skirting around the issues at stake. If someone had done a bad piece of work, it was stated very forwardly, like "This is a waste of time" and we'd move on. It's not like that any more, it's very gentle. *Miraj Ahmed (Architectural Association/ Cambridge University)*

× The thing that I miss about how it used to be is that people were prepared to care and they had an opinion. That has been softened, to the extreme in a lot of ways. It's often hard to tell if people care about each other's work. *Kelly Chorpening (Camberwell College of Arts)*

× I think that there has been a gradual and very positive change in teaching and in society in the last 25 years. There has been a shift in a patriarchal society and the power dominated male teaching structure, to an equal gender mix in teaching. When I studied there was only an aggressive male voice in the crit. Also, I knew tutors thought my work was good, but I had no idea why. There was no critical forum, no way I could have accessed that at all. So when I started teaching it was a wonderful opportunity to try and understand all of these things. *Ann Hulland (Kingston University)*

- Going back 30 years we never talked about our work in any kind of group situation at all; there were none. That was one of the things that I did when I started teaching here as I thought that this had got to change. Staff had a very limited vocabulary back then and it was very formal. People would use code words. If a sculpture or a painting was reasonably good, you would say, "It's looking well", but that would be about it, you would not expand on that. It was very much the attitude that there was a mystery to art. Postmodernism had not really kicked in and so maintaining that mystery was vital! Whereas now we try a great deal to demystify it and talk about what is actually there. It's a whole change of attitude. *David Moore (Edinburgh College of Art)*

FURTHER RESOURCES

To view the supporting video and find/submit additional learning resources on the topic of crits, visit:

WWW.Q-ART.ORG.UK